Table of Contents

Introduction

Caribbean Sea, suboceanic basin of the western Atlantic Ocean, lying between latitudes 9° and 22° N and longitudes 89° and 60° W. It is approximately 1,063,000 square miles (2,753,000 square km) in extent. To the south it is bounded by the coasts of Venezuela, Colombia, and Panama; to the west by Costa Rica, Nicaragua, Honduras, Guatemala, Belize, and the Yucatán Peninsula of Mexico; to the north by the Greater Antilles islands of Cuba, Hispaniola, Jamaica, and Puerto Rico; and to the east by the north-south chain of the Lesser Antilles, consisting of the island arc that extends from the Virgin Islands in the northeast to Trinidad, off the Venezuelan coast, in the southeast. Within the boundaries of the Caribbean itself, Jamaica, to the south of Cuba, is the largest of a number of islands.

The Caribbean is a diverse region with significant economic potential and growth opportunities. Gross National Income (GNI) per capita varies from around US$800 to over US$30,000 and some countries rely on commodity exports, while others on tourism.

With its stunning scenery and vibrant cultures, the Caribbean is one of the world's top tourist destinations. Sustainable use of ocean resources, known as the "blue economy," offers great economic growth potential, as well as further development of the region's services, logistics, agriculture, creative, and digital sectors.

Many small economies, including those that are tourism-dependent, were maintaining a positive growth rate prior to the onset of the COVID-19 pandemic. The Caribbean has been badly impacted by the near halt in tourism. The Caribbean economy is anticipated to contract by 1.8% in 2020, and by 3.1% excluding Guyana. Many jobs are affected, and a recent high frequency phone survey in one of the Caribbean small states suggests that poverty headcounts are rising, though the magnitude and duration of this increase will depend on the pace of economic recovery.

Together with the Gulf of Mexico, the Caribbean Sea has been erroneously termed the American Mediterranean, owing to the fact that, like the Mediterranean Sea, it is located between two continental landmasses. In neither hydrology nor climate, however, does the Caribbean resemble the Mediterranean. The preferred oceanographic term for the Caribbean is the Antillean-Caribbean Sea, which, together with the Gulf of Mexico, forms the Central American Sea. The Caribbean's greatest known depth is Cayman Trench (Bartlett Deep) between Cuba and Jamaica, approximately 25,216 feet (7,686 metres) below sea level.

Physical Features
Geology

The geologic age of the Caribbean is not known with certainty. As part of the Central American Sea, it is presumed to have been connected with the Mediterranean during Paleozoic times (i.e., about 541 to 252 million years ago) and then gradually to have separated from it as the Atlantic Ocean was formed. The ancient sediments overlying the seafloor of the Caribbean, as well as of the Gulf of Mexico, are about a half mile (about one kilometre) in thickness, with the upper strata representing sediments from the Mesozoic and Cenozoic eras (from about 252 million years ago to the present) and the lower strata presumably representing sediments of the Paleozoic and Mesozoic eras (from about 541 to 66 million years ago). Three phases of sedimentation have been identified. During the first and second phases the basin was free of deformation. The Central American Sea apparently became separated from the Atlantic before the end of the first phase. Near the end of the second phase, gentle warping and faulting occurred, forming the Aves and Beata ridges. Forces producing the Panamanian isthmus and the Antillean arc were vertical, resulting in no ultimate horizontal movement. The sediment beds tend to arch in the middle of the basins and to dip as landmasses are approached. The younger Cenozoic beds (formed during the last 65 million years) are generally horizontal, having been laid down after the deformations occurred. Connections were established with the Pacific Ocean during the Cretaceous Period (from about 145 to 66 million years ago) but were broken when the land bridges that permitted mammals to cross between North and South America were formed in the Miocene and Pliocene epochs (about 23 to 2.6 million years ago).

The existing sediment cover of the seabed consists of red clay in the deep basins and trenches, globigerina ooze (a calcareous marine deposit) on the rises, and pteropod ooze on the ridges and continental slopes. Clay minerals appear to have been washed down by the Amazon and Orinoco rivers, as well as by the Magdalena River in Colombia. Coral reefs fringe most of the islands.

Physiography

The Caribbean Sea is divided into five submarine basins, each roughly elliptical in shape, which are separated from one another by submerged ridges and rises. These are the Yucatán, Cayman, Colombian, Venezuelan, and Grenada basins. The northernmost of these, the Yucatán Basin, is separated from the Gulf of Mexico by the Yucatán Channel, which runs between Cuba and the Yucatán Peninsula and has a sill depth (i.e., the depth of the submarine ridge between basins) of about 5,250 feet (1,600 metres). The Cayman Basin, to the south, is partially separated from the Yucatán Basin by Cayman Ridge, an incomplete fingerlike ridge that extends from the southern part of Cuba toward Guatemala, rising above the surface at one point to form the Cayman Islands. The Nicaraguan Rise, a wide triangular ridge with a sill depth of about 4,000 feet (1,200 metres), extends from Honduras and Nicaragua to Hispaniola, bearing the island of Jamaica and separating the Cayman Basin from the Colombian Basin. The Colombian Basin is partly separated from the Venezuelan Basin by the Beata Ridge. The basins are connected by the submerged Aruba Gap at depths greater than 13,000 feet (4,000 metres). The Aves Ridge, incomplete at its southern extremity, separates the Venezuelan Basin from the small Grenada Basin, which is bounded to the east by the Antillean arc of islands.

Subsurface water enters the Caribbean Sea across two sills. These sills are located below the Anegada Passage, which runs between the Virgin Islands and the Lesser Antilles, and the Windward Passage, which stretches between Cuba and Hispaniola. The sill depth of Anegada Passage is between 6,400 and 7,700 feet (1,950 and 2,350 metres), whereas that of the Windward Passage is between 5,250 and 5,350 feet (1,600 and 1,630 metres).

Hydrology

North Atlantic deep water enters the Caribbean beneath the Windward Passage and is characterized by its rich oxygen content and by a salinity of slightly less than 35 parts per thousand. From there it divides to fill the Yucatán, Cayman, and Colombian basins at depths near 6,500 feet (2,000 metres). This Caribbean bottom water also enters the Venezuelan Basin, thus introducing high-oxygen water at depths of 5,900 to 9,800 feet (1,800 to 3,000 metres). Subantarctic intermediate water (i.e., water differing in several characteristics from the surface and bottom layers of water that it separates) enters the Caribbean below the Anegada Passage at depths of 1,600 to 3,300 feet (500 to 1,000 metres). Above this water, the subtropical undercurrent and surface water enter. The shallow sill depths of the Antillean arc block the entry of Antarctic bottom water, so that the bottom temperature of the Caribbean Sea is close to

39 °F (4 °C), as compared with the Atlantic bottom temperature of less than 36 °F (2 °C).

Surface currents, bearing both high- and low-salinity water depending on the source, enter the Caribbean mainly through the channels and passages of the southern Antilles. These waters are then forced by the trade winds through the narrow Yucatán Channel into the Gulf of Mexico. The wind-driven surface water accumulates in the Yucatán Basin and the Gulf of Mexico, where it results in a higher average sea level than in the Atlantic, forming a hydrostatic head that is believed to constitute the main driving force of the Gulf Stream. Of the water passing through the Yucatán Channel each second, only about one-fourth represents the deeper Subantarctic intermediate water. The remainder is the surface water that passed over the Antillean arc at depths of less than 2,600 feet (800 metres).

Climate

The climate of the Caribbean generally is tropical, but there are great local variations, depending on mountain elevation, water currents, and the trade winds. Rainfall varies from about 10 inches (25 cm) per year on the island of Bonaire off the coast of Venezuela to some 350 inches (900 cm) annually in parts of Dominica. The northeast trade winds dominate the region with an average velocity of 10 to 20 miles (16 to 32 km) per hour. Tropical storms reaching a hurricane velocity of more than 75 miles (120 km) per hour are seasonally common in the northern Caribbean as well as in the Gulf of Mexico; they are almost nonexistent in the far south. The hurricane season is from June to November, but hurricanes occur most frequently in September. The yearly average is about eight such storms. The Caribbean has fewer hurricanes than either the western Pacific (where these storms are called typhoons) or the Gulf of Mexico. Most hurricanes form in the eastern Atlantic near the Cape Verde Islands and follow the path of the trade winds into the Caribbean and the Gulf of Mexico, although the exact path of any hurricane is unpredictable. In 1963 one of the deadliest hurricanes on record, Flora, caused the loss of more than 7,000 lives and extensive property damage in the Caribbean alone. Such storms also have been a major cause of crop failure in the region.

Caribbean cuisine

Caribbean cuisine is a fusion of African, Creole, Cajun, Amerindian, European, Latin American, Indian/South Asian, Middle Eastern, and Chinese. These traditions were brought from many different countries when they came to the Caribbean. In addition, the population has created styles that are unique to the region.

Caribbean dishes

Ingredients that are common in most islands' dishes are rice, plantains, beans, cassava, cilantro, bell peppers, chickpeas, tomatoes, sweet potatoes, coconut, and any of various meats that are locally available like beef, poultry, pork or fish. A characteristic seasoning for the region is a green herb-and-oil-based marinade called sofrito, which imparts a flavor profile which is quintessentially Caribbean in character. Ingredients may include garlic, onions, scotch bonnet peppers, celery, green onions, and herbs like cilantro, Mexican mint, chives, marjoram, rosemary, tarragon and thyme. This green seasoning is used for a variety of dishes like curries, stews and roasted meats.

Traditional dishes are so important to regional culture that, for example, the local version of Caribbean goat stew has been chosen as the official national dish of Montserrat and is also one of the signature dishes of St. Kitts and Nevis. Another popular dish in the Anglophone Caribbean is called "cook-up", or pelau. Ackee and saltfish is another popular dish that is unique to Jamaica. Callaloo is a dish containing leafy vegetables such as spinach and sometimes okra amongst others, widely distributed in the Caribbean, with a distinctively mixed African and indigenous character.

The variety of dessert dishes in the area also reflects the mixed origins of the recipes. In some areas, black cake, a derivative of English Christmas pudding, may be served, especially on special occasions.

Over time, food from the Caribbean has evolved into a narrative technique through which their culture has been accentuated and promoted. However, by studying Caribbean culture through a literary lens there then runs the risk of generalizing exoticist ideas about food practices from the tropics. Some food theorists argue that this depiction of Caribbean food in various forms of media contributes to the inaccurate conceptions revolving around their culinary practices, which are much more grounded in unpleasant historical events. Therefore, it can be argued that the connection between the idea of the Caribbean being the ultimate paradise and Caribbean food being exotic is based on inaccurate information.

Recipes

Jamaican rum punch

Ingredients

- white rum 250ml
- dark or coconut rum 150ml
- strawberry-flavoured syrup or grenadine 200ml
- pineapple juice 250ml
- orange juice 250ml
- limes 4, juiced (about 100ml)
- nutmeg a pinch, freshly grated
- Angostura bitters a dash, (optional)
- orange, lemon and lime slices to serve

Method

STEP 1

Tip all the ingredients except the fruit slices into a large pitcher. Stir and add plenty of crushed ice, finishing with the fruit slices to serve.

Caribbean chicken stew

1 Hour 10 Minutes + Marinating Serves 4-6Easy

Caribbean chicken stew comes flavoured with thyme, ginger, lime, Angoustura bitters and scotch bonnet sauce. Serve with coconut rice and peas

 Ingredients

- whole chicken thighs and drumsticks (skin on) 8-12
- caster sugar 5 tbsp

GREEN SEASONING

- spring onions 2
- thyme 3 sprigs, leaves only
- coriander leaves chopped to make 2 tbsp

- flat-leaf parsley leaves chopped to make 1 tbsp
- ginger chopped to make 1 tsp
- garlic 2 cloves, peeled
- vegetable oil a small glug
- lime ½, juiced
- Angostura bitters a generous dash
- scotch bonnet pepper sauce a couple of dashes

COCONUT RICE AND PEAS

- vegetable oil 1 tbsp
- onion 1, finely chopped
- garlic 2 cloves, crushed
- thyme 1 sprig
- ground allspice ½ tsp
- basmati rice 500g, rinsed
- coconut milk 400ml tin
- vegetable stock 600ml
- scotch bonnet pepper 1
- kidney beans 400g tin, drained

Method

STEP 1

To make the green seasoning, pulse all the ingredients with a little salt and pepper in a blender or food processor until finely chopped. Put the chicken into a bowl, add the green seasoning, mix well and leave to marinade for at least 4 hours or ideally overnight.

STEP 2

When you are ready to cook, brush any excess marinade from the chicken back into the bowl and keep. Evenly spread the sugar in a large, wide, heavy-based pan and melt over a medium heat – don't take your eyes off the pot, give it a stir and wait for the sugar to change from golden to dark brown. As soon as it does, the sugar should be bubbling and just smoking – immediately add the chicken and cook for 10 minutes, allowing the chicken to darken and caramelise on all sides.

STEP 3

Reduce the heat, pour any remaining marinade into the pan, along with a little seasoning, give it a stir, put the lid on and leave to stew for 30-40 minutes, stirring now and again, until the chicken is cooked through. Add a splash of water if it gets a little dry.

STEP 4

To make the rice, heat the oil in a large pan over a low heat and soften the onion with a little salt for 2-5 minutes, stirring regularly. Add the garlic, thyme and allspice, and cook for 30 seconds, stirring continuously, until the aromas are released. Add the rice and stir until the grains are well coated, followed by the coconut milk, stock, scotch bonnet, kidney beans and a good pinch of salt. Bring it to the boil and cook for 10 minutes. Reduce the heat to a simmer and continue to cook until the rice is just tender and the liquid is absorbed – you may need to add a little extra just-boiled water to ensure the rice is fully cooked.

STEP 5

Remove the thyme sprig and the scotch bonnet from the rice, fluff it up with a fork, trying to gently fold through the kidney beans, and season to taste.

STEP 6

Serve the chicken with the rice and peas, with a drizzle of the gravy over everything and some drops of scotch bonnet pepper sauce.

Banana and rum fritters

45 Minutes Makes 20-30Easy

Try this popular French Caribbean sweet snack, enjoyed on Sundays around carnival time. We think they're delicious any time of year

Ingredients

- ripe bananas 4
- golden granulated sugar 60g
- eggs 2
- dessicated coconut 1 tbsp (optional)
- plain flour 125g
- baking powder 1 tsp
- vanilla pod 1, cut in half lengthwise
- lime 1, zested
- ground cinnamon 1 pinch
- ground nutmeg 1 pinch
- white rum 1 tbsp
- sunflower oil
- icing sugar 1 tbsp

Method

STEP 1

Peel the bananas, put them in a bowl and mash with a fork. Whisk in the sugar and eggs, then the coconut (if using), flour and baking powder. Using a small knife, scrape the seeds from the vanilla pod and add to the mixture, then stir in the lime zest, cinnamon, nutmeg and rum.

STEP 2

In a deep pan, heat some oil (filling a pan no more than 1/3 full) over a medium heat until it reaches 180C, or until a cube of bread browns in 30–40 seconds. Make sure the oil doesn't get too hot and start to smoke. Gently drop tbsps of the batter into the oil and cook for about 2 minutes on each side, turning occasionally, until dark golden all over.

STEP 3

Scoop the fritters out of the oil and drain on paper towels. Sprinkle with icing sugar and serve hot.

Antiguan ducana

Ingredients

- fresh banana leaves for wrapping
- plain flour 100g
- cornmeal 150g
- dark brown muscovado sugar 60g
- ground cinnamon 2 tsp
- nutmeg grated to make 1 tsp
- pumpkin or sweet potato 120g, finely grated
- fresh or desiccated coconut 100g, finely grated
- evaporated milk 120ml
- vanilla extract 1 tsp
- butter 2 tbsp, softened
- raisins or sultanas 50g

- vegetable oil for the banana leaves

Method

STEP 1

Prepare the banana leaves by cutting them into 30cm x 20cm pieces, then rinse and set aside to dry.

STEP 2

Mix the flour, cornmeal, sugar, cinnamon, nutmeg and ½ tsp of salt in a bowl, then add the grated pumpkin and coconut, and combine well. Gradually add the milk and vanilla extract, mixing while you pour to avoid any lumps, until a wet mixture forms. Fold in the butter, followed by the raisins. Chill until you are ready to fill the banana leaves.

STEP 3

Prepare the steamer and let the water start to boil on a low-medium heat.

STEP 4

To fill the banana leaves, put a prepared leaf on a flat surface, pour a little oil on your hands, then rub lightly onto the leaf. Add a few spoonfuls of the mixture into the centre of the leaf. Shape the dough into a log shape with your hands, keeping it in the centre of the leaf. To seal, fold the longest horizontal sides into the centre, covering the dough entirely, then fold both ends into the centre. Tie across the centre of the parcel in a cross shape using kitchen string to ensure there are no open sides.

STEP 5

Repeat until all the mixture is used up, then put the parcels inside the steamer on top of each other for 30-40 minutes.

STEP 6

The ducana are ready when the dough is opaque and slightly firm. Enjoy by themselves or with stewed saltfish and antruba (chopped okra with aubergine).

Nutritional Information

Kcals

435

Fat

17.2g

Saturates

11.2g

Carbs

59.1g

Sugars

22.9g

Fibre

5g

Protein

8.1g

Salt

0.7g

Jerk seasoning mix

Ingredients

- allspice berries 1 tbsp
- black peppercorns 2 tsp
- ground cinnamon 1 tsp
- dried thyme 2 tsp
- cayenne pepper 2 tsp
- garlic granules 1 tsp

Method

STEP 1

Put the whole spices in a small pan and heat until fragrant, stirring so they don't burn. Cool, then grind with a spice grinder or pestle and mortar. Stir in remaining spices and store in an airtight jar.

Kept in a small airtight jar, these spice blends will last for 2 months.

Dressed crab (Crabe farci)

40 Minutes Serves4

Boil crab with bay leaves and salt or buy fresh crabmeat to create this essential element in any assiette Creole (Creole platter)

Ingredients

- baguette 70g (about ¼ of a baguette), slightly stale

- semi-skimmed milk 3 tbsp

- spring onions 2, roughly chopped

- onion 1, chopped

- garlic 3 cloves

- flat-leaf parsley 2 sprigs

- thyme 1 sprig, leaves picked

- red habanero or scotch bonnet) ½ chilli, seeded

- butter 2 tbsp

- mixed crabmeat 175g, shredded

- lime 1, juiced

- fine dried breadcrumbs 3 tbsp

- lime wedges to serve

Method

STEP 1

Heat the oven to 180C/fan 160C/gas 4. Soak the baguette in the milk for 10 minutes.

STEP 2

Put the spring onions, onion, garlic, parsley, thyme, and chilli in a food processor and blend until very finely chopped.

STEP 3

Melt the butter in a frying pan.Add the chopped onion mixture and cook for a minute.Add the crabmeat and lime juice and cook for 2 minutes, then remove from the heat.

STEP 4

Squeeze the milk out of the bread. Put the bread in a food processor and blend to a purée.Add the bread to the crab. Put the pan over a medium heat and cook for 3–4 minutes, stirring regularly so it doesn't stick to the pan. Season and remove from the heat.

STEP 5

Put the stuffing in small ramekins (if you used a whole crab, fill the cleaned shell with the stuffing) and sprinkle the breadcrumbs over. Put in the oven for 10 minutes, or until golden. Serve hot, on its own, or with salad.

Jamaican curry pork

5 Hours 30 Minutes Serves 4-6

A spin on the classic curry goat, this spiced pork curry is melt-in-the-mouth and full of Caribbean flavour

Ingredients

- vegetable oil for frying
- onions 2, finely chopped
- pork shoulder 1kg, fat trimmed, and diced
- allspice berries ground to make 2 heaped tsp
- medium curry powder 3 tbsp
- paprika (not smoked) 1 tbsp
- ground coriander 1 tbsp

- celery salt 1 tbsp

- garlic granules 1 tbsp

- thyme 4-5 sprigs, leaves picked

- black peppercorns ground to make ¼ tsp

- garlic 6 large cloves, thinly sliced

- scotch bonnet chillies 1-2, pierced but left whole

- plum tomatoes 4, roughly chopped

- spring onions 4, thinly sliced

RICE AND PEAS

- vegetable oil 1 tbsp

- onion 1, finely chopped

- garlic 4 large cloves, thinly sliced

- long-grain rice 300g

- butter 25g

- thyme 4-5 sprigs

- gungo peas or kidney beans 400g tin, drained (see notes below)

- coconut milk 300ml

Method

STEP 1

Heat a large pan over a medium-high heat, pour in enough oil to coat the base and cook the onions for 15 minutes or until translucent. Add the pork, spices, thyme and black pepper, and stir well, coating the meat. Add the garlic, chillies, tomatoes and most of the spring onions (keep a little back for garnishing), mix well and pour in 1 litre of cold water to cover the ingredients. Bring to the boil, reduce the heat to low and simmer gently for 2½-3 hours, stirring occasionally and adding a splash of water if it looks a little dry, until the pork is tender.

STEP 2

For the rice and peas, put a lidded pan over a medium heat with the vegetable oil and cook the onion for 10 minutes until soft. Add the garlic and cook for a minute before adding the rice, butter, thyme, beans and a generous amount of seasoning. Mix well, ensuring the rice is coated in the mixture, then add the coconut milk and 175ml of cold water, stirring well. Cover and cook gently for 20 minutes, then remove the lid and cook for a further 15 minutes until the liquid is fully evaporated. Fluff the rice with a fork and serve with the curry pork and reserved spring onions.

Gungo or pigeon peas are the traditional bean used in the Caribbean dish rice and peas. They are available from large supermarkets – look out for Dunn's River or Tropical Sun brands.

Papacoco (bavaroise à la papaye)

Ingredients

- papayas 2 large ripe, halved and seeds scooped out
- coconut milk 600ml
- white rhum agricole or white rum 400ml
- ground cinnamon a pinch
- vanilla extract 1 tsp

Method

STEP 1

Blend the papaya flesh with the coconut milk in a blender, then pour through a sieve into a bowl. Add the rum, cinnamon and vanilla and stir.

STEP 2

Transfer to a cocktail shaker and shake well, or pour into a large jug and whisk vigorously. Put some ice cubes into each glass and pour in the cocktail. Drink immediately, before the papaya starts to separate from the milk.

Caribbean fish curry

Check out our vibrant fish curry recipe with Caribbean curry powder, punchy Scotch bonnet chillies and creamy coconut milk

Ingredients

- skinless white fish fillets 4 large
- lemon ½, juiced
- mild Caribbean curry powder 2 tbsp
- groundnut oil 1 tbsp
- spring onions 1 bunch, sliced
- ginger a small chunk, finely grated
- garlic 2 cloves, crushed
- scotch bonnet chilli 1, finely chopped
- red pepper 1, chopped into chunks
- thyme 1 tsp of leaves, chopped, plus extra to serve
- coconut milk 400g tin
- cooked rice to serve

Method

STEP 1

Rub the fish with the lemon juice, 1 tsp of the curry powder and some seasoning, and leave to sit while you make the sauce. Heat the oil in a shallow casserole or deep frying pan with a lid. Cook the spring onions, ginger, garlic, chilli and pepper for 5 minutes, then stir in the remaining curry powder and thyme and cook for 1 minute. Add the coconut milk and simmer, uncovered, for 10 minutes until the sauce has thickened.

STEP 2

Add the fish, pushing down into the sauce, then cover with a lid and simmer gently for 8-10 minutes or until the fish flakes easily. Scatter with a little fresh thyme and serve with rice.

Jamaican goat curry

Ingredients

- diced kid goat meat 400g
- Jamaican curry powder (try Dunn's River) 4 tbsp
- garlic 4 cloves, and 2 crushed
- oil for frying
- onion 1 large, chopped
- scotch bonnet chilli 1, seeded and finely chopped
- thyme 3 sprigs, leaves picked
- tomatoes 4, roughly chopped
- light chicken stock 600ml
- waxy potatoes 300g, peeledand cut into chunks
- rice to serve

Method

STEP 1

The day before, mix the goat meat with 2 tbsp of the curry powder, the whole bashed garlic cloves, a good grinding of black pepper and 1 tsp salt. Cover and leave to marinate overnight.

STEP 2

The next day, heat the oven to 160C/fan 140C/gas 3. Add 2 tbsp oil to a large ovenproof pan with a lid. Add the marinated meat in batches, discarding the whole garlic, and brown all over. Scoop out onto a plate once browned.

STEP 3

Add the crushed garlic, onion and scotch bonnet to the pan and cook for 7-8 minutes until softened.

STEP 4

Return the meat to the pan with the thyme leaves, tomatoes and stock. Put on a lid and transfer to the oven for 2½ hours.

STEP 5

Stir in the potatoes and cook for another 30 minutes. Serve with rice.

Jerk chicken skewers with mango salad

Coat chicken pieces with jerk seasoning and cook over a hot griddle pan for some midweek heat ready in 20 minutes. Serve with a refreshing mango, pepper and sugar snap pea salad.

Ingredients

- chicken breasts 2, cut into bite-sized pieces
- jerk seasoning 1 tbsp

- olive oil 2 tsp, plus 1 tbsp for the salad

- limes 2, juiced

- red onion ½

- sugar snap peas a handful

- red pepper 1, chopped

- little gem lettuce 1, cut into chunky pieces

- mango ½, cubed

Method

STEP 1

Tip the chicken pieces into a bowl and season generously, then add the jerk seasoning, 2 tsp of oil and the juice of 1 lime, and toss really well. Divide the chicken pieces between 4 small metal skewers. Heat a griddle pan over a medium-high heat and cook the skewers for 5-6 minutes on each side until charred and cooked through.

STEP 2

Meanwhile, grate the onion into a bowl and add the juice of 1 lime, 1 tbsp of oil and a little seasoning. Tip in the remaining ingredients and mix well.

STEP 3

Divide the salad between 2 plates and serve with the skewers.

The classic mojito

The mojito was the cocktail you told us you most wanted the recipe for, and we're not surprised as it is such a classic. Very refreshing and sure to whisk you away to the Caribbean!

Ingredients

- fresh mint leaves 10, plus a sprig to garnish
- white sugar 3 tsp
- Havana Club 3 Años rum 50ml
- soda to top up

- Angostura bitters 3 drops

Method

STEP 1

In a tumbler, muddle the mint leaves with the sugar. Pour over the rum and stir. Add a handful of ice cubes, top with soda and stir again, then add the Angostura Bitters and garnish with a mint sprig.

Jamaican pepperpot stew

This Jamaican pepperpot stew recipe is an easy one-pot to feed the family. Ginger, chilli and allspice spice up the tender beef and sweet potato for a winter warming dish.

Ingredients

- braising or stewing beef such as shin, cut into small pieces

- oil for frying

- onions 2 small, chopped

- ginger a large walnut-sized piece, peeled and chopped

- garlic 1 clove, crushed

- scotch bonnet chilli 1, seeded and finely chopped

- dried thyme 1/2 tsp

- allspice berries 8

- cinnamon stick 1

- beef stock 800ml

- coconut milk 400g tin

- sweet potatoes 300g, peeled and cut into 2-3cm chunks

- spinach 250g, washed and chopped

Method

STEP 1

Heat a large casserole and fry the beef in 2 tbsp oil until browned. Add the onion and cook until soft then tip in the

ginger, garlic and chilli and cook for a couple of minutes.
Add the thyme, allspice, cinnamon, stock and coconut milk.
Bring up to

a gentle simmer, cover then cook for 1½ hours.

STEP 2

Add the sweet potato and cook uncovered until just tender,
about 20 minutes. Stir in the spinach and simmer for a good 5
minutes. Serve in bowls.

Jamaican prawn, pepper and coconut stew

This recipe for Jamaican prawn, pepper and coconut stew is
easy to make and ready in just 30 minutes. Plus, it's gluten-
free and under 500 calories.

Ingredients

- spring onions 6, chopped (including the green bits)
- ginger a small chunk, finely chopped
- garlic 1 clove, crushed
- scotch bonnet chilli 1, finely chopped
- olive oil
- ground allspice 1/2 tsp
- thyme 1/4 tsp of leaves, chopped
- red pepper 1, seeded and chopped
- half-fat coconut milk 400g tin
- spinach 100g, chopped
- raw peeled prawns 150g
- basmati rice 100g

Method

STEP 1

Cook ¾ of the spring onion, all of the ginger, garlic and chilli in a little oil for 5 minutes, then stir in the allspice and thyme and cook for a minute. Add the pepper and coconut milk and simmer for 10 minutes.

STEP 2

Stir in the spinach and prawns and cook for a few more minutes, until prawns are pink. Cook the rice, then serve with the stew and a scattering of the remaining spring onions.

Jamaican ginger and caramel cake

Ingredients

- salted butter 250g, diced, plus extra for the tin
- black treacle 200g
- dark rum 100ml
- whole milk 200ml
- dark brown muscovado sugar 100g
- stoned dates 200g, roughly chopped

- stem ginger 3 balls, roughly chopped plus 1 tbsp syrup from the jar for drizzle
- Carnation caramel 150g, plus 4 tbsp for the icing
- eggs 3
- gluten-free plain flour 400g
- bicarbonate of soda 2 tsp
- ground ginger 2 tbsp
- ground cinnamon 2 tsp
- mixed spice 1 tsp

ICING

- salted butter 150g
- golden icing sugar 450g
- vanilla extract 1 tsp

DRIZZLE

- Caramac bars 3 x 30g bars

Method

STEP 1

Heat the oven to 160C/fan 140C/gas 3. Butter and line 2 x 20cm springform tins with baking paper.

STEP 2

Put the treacle, rum, milk and muscovado sugar in a pan with the chopped dates and stem ginger chunks. Bring to the boil, then bubble for 3 minutes to soften the dates. Use a hand blender to blitz the date mixture to a smooth purée – be careful, it will be hot! Stir in the diced butter until it's melted, followed by the caramel and the eggs.

STEP 3

Combine the flour, bicarb and spices in a bowl, then make a well in the centre and pour in the warm date mixture. Mix with a wooden spoon until the batter is lump-free. Divide between the two tins (weigh the mixture for really even layers), then bake in the centre of the oven for 1 hour or until a skewer poked into the centre comes out clean. Cool in the tins.

STEP 4

When the cakes are cool (or, if wrapped in clingfilm, the sponges will mature to an even tastier cake in a day or two) remove from the tins and make the icing. Beat the butter with electric beaters until soft, then beat in half the icing sugar. Beat in the remaining icing sugar with the vanilla extract, until the icing is fluffy and pale. Beat in the 4 tbsp caramel. Spread a thick layer of icing over one of the cakes and chill for 20 minutes to firm up, then sandwich the second cake on top. Spread the rest of the icing sparsely over the top and sides of the cake, filling any gaps where the sponges were sandwiched and scraping excess icing to give straight, clean, 'naked' sides. Chill for 30 minutes until the icing is cold and firm.

STEP 5

Break up the Caramac bars and melt with the ginger syrup. Remove the cake from the fridge and spoon over the melted sauce a spoon at a time, letting it run down the edges of the cake. It should cool and harden as it hits the cold icing, resulting in dribbles that stop before they hit the bottom of the cake.

Caribbean-style lamb curry

Ingredients

- lamb neck fillet 750g, trimmed and cut into chunks
- lime 1, juiced plus wedges to serve
- mild curry powder 2 tbsp
- flavourless oil
- onion 1, halved and sliced
- garlic 3 cloves, crushed
- ginger a 2.5cm piece, peeled and grated
- scotch bonnet chillies 2, seeded and finely chopped

- ground allspice 2 tsp

- ground cloves 1 tsp

- dried thyme 1 tsp

- cinnamon stick 1/2

- chopped tomatoes 400g tin

- brown sugar 1 tbsp, (any kind)

- chicken stock cube or concentrated

- steamed rice to serve

Method

STEP 1

Put the lamb in a bowl with the lime juice, 1 tbsp curry powder and lots of seasoning. Toss and leave to sit.

STEP 2

Heat 1 tbsp oil in a frying pan and fry the onion, garlic, ginger and chilli for 5 minutes. Stir in the rest of the curry powder, allspice, cloves, thyme and cinnamon and cook for a minute. Add the lamb and fry for 5 minutes. Add the tomatoes and sugar. Refill the tomato tin with water and stir this in. Add a chicken stock cube. Bring to a simmer, cover and cook for 1 hour. Remove the lid and simmer for a further 30 minutes, stirring regularly towards the end. Serve with steamed rice and lime wedges.

Creole pork ragoût (Ragout de cochon)

Ingredients

- skinless pork shoulder 700g, cut into chunks
- limes 2, juiced
- garlic 4 cloves, very finely chopped
- ground allspice 2 tsp
- vegetable oil
- onions 2, sliced
- spring onions 2, chopped
- thyme 2 sprigs

- bay leaves 2
- clove 1
- red habanero or scotch bonnet or chilli 1

Method

STEP 1

Marinate the pork, in the fridge, overnight with the juice of 1 lime, half the garlic, half the allspice, salt and pepper.

STEP 2

Heat the oven to 160C/fan 140C/gas 3. Remove the pork from the marinade and pat dry with paper towels. Heat 2 tbsp oil in a large, heavy pan over a medium–high heat, fry the pork until it is browned all over.Add the onions, spring onions, the remaining allspice, salt and pepper, stir and brown for a few minutes.

STEP 3

Add the juice of 1 lime, the remaining garlic, thyme sprigs, bay leaves, clove, the whole chilli and 125ml water. Cover and put in the oven for 2 hours, until the meat is very tender. Serve with stewed pigeon peas and rice, or a vegetable gratin.

Caribbean beef patties

Ingredients

- drizzle of oil
- 1 small onion , finely chopped
- 2 garlic cloves , crushed
- 250g beef mince
- 1 potato , cut into 1cm/0.5in cubes
- 2 tsp turmeric
- 2 tbsp tomato purée
- few thyme sprigs
- 2 tbsp hot pepper sauce
- 500g block shortcrust pastry

- 1 egg , beaten

- green salad , to serve

Method

STEP 1

Heat the oil in a pan, add the onion and cook for 5 mins. Add the garlic and beef, turn up the heat and cook until the meat is browned. Add the potato, half the turmeric, the purée and thyme, plus 200ml water. Cover and simmer for 15 mins, then remove the lid and cook for 5 mins more. Add the hot pepper sauce and leave to cool.

STEP 2

Heat oven to 220C/200C fan/gas 7. Roll out the pastry to the thickness of a £1 coin. Cut out 6 x 15cm circles, using a small plate as a guide. Divide the mince between the circles, piling it up on one side. Mix the egg with the remaining turmeric, brush around the edge of each circle, then fold over and use a fork to seal the edges. Arrange on a baking tray lined with baking parchment, brush with a little more egg and bake for 20-25 mins. Serve with a green salad.

GOES WELL WITH

Rum & coconut treacle tart

Exotic avocado salad

Reggae reggae nachos

Rum punch

Ingredients

- 175ml freshly squeezed orange juice
- 75ml freshly squeezed lime juice
- 150ml good-quality golden rum
- 50ml sugar syrup
- dash of grenadine syrup
- dash of Angostura bitters

- ice cubes, to serve

- generous pinch of freshly grated nutmeg

- 2 thick slices orange, to garnish

- maraschino cherries, to garnish

Method

STEP 1

Pour the juices, rum, sugar syrup, grenadine and Angostura bitters into a large jug and give it a good stir. Pop into the fridge to chill for 1 hr.

STEP 2

Serve over ice cubes, sprinkle over the nutmeg and garnish with an orange slice and maraschino cherry, speared with a cocktail stick.

Sticky jerk salmon with mango slaw

Ingredients

- 2 heaped tbsp Jamaican jerk paste
- 2 tbsp clear honey
- 4 salmon fillets
- juice 2 limes
- ½ red cabbage , core removed, thinly sliced
- 1 firm but ripe mango , skin removed, thinly sliced
- 1 red pepper , thinly sliced
- 6 spring onions , thinly sliced on an angle
- small bunch coriander , leaves picked

Method

STEP 1

Heat the grill to medium-high. Mix the jerk paste and 1 tbsp honey together in a bowl. Place the salmon fillets on a foil-lined baking tray and brush all over with the sauce. Cook on the top shelf for 8-10 mins or until just cooked through (move the tray down a shelf if the salmon starts getting too caramelised).

STEP 2

Meanwhile, put the remaining honey, lime juice and some seasoning in a large bowl and mix together. Add the red cabbage, mango, pepper, spring onions and coriander, and toss through the dressing. Serve the salmon on a pile of the slaw.

Jerk chicken with rice & peas

Ingredients

- 12 chicken thighs, bone in
- 1 lime, halved
- hot sauce, to serve (optional)
- For the marinade
- 1 big bunch spring onions, roughly chopped

- thumb-sized piece ginger, roughly chopped

- 3 garlic cloves

- ½ a small onion

- 3 scotch bonnet chillies, deseeded if you want less heat

- ½ tsp dried thyme, or 1 tbsp thyme leaves

- 1 lime, juiced

- 2 tbsp soy sauce

- 2 tbsp vegetable oil

- 3 tbsp brown sugar

- 1 tbsp ground allspice

For the rice & peas

- 200g basmati rice

- 400g can coconut milk

- 1 bunch spring onions, sliced

- 2 large thyme sprigs

- 2 garlic cloves, finely chopped

- 1 tsp ground allspice

- 2 x 410g cans kidney beans, drained

Method

STEP 1

To make the jerk marinade, combine the spring onions, ginger, garlic, onion, scotch bonnet chillies, dried thyme, lime juice, soy sauce, vegetable oil, brown sugar and ground allspice in a food processor along with 1 tsp salt, and blend to a purée. If you're having trouble getting it to blend, just keep turning off the blender, stirring the mixture, and trying again. Eventually it will start to blend up – don't be tempted to add water, as you want a thick paste.

STEP 2

Taste the jerk mixture for seasoning – it should taste pretty salty, but not unpleasantly, puckering salty. You can now throw in more chillies if it's not spicy enough for you. If it tastes too salty and sour, try adding in a bit more brown sugar until the mixture tastes well balanced.

STEP 3

Make a few slashes in 12 chicken thighs and pour the marinade over the meat, rubbing it into all the crevices. Cover and leave to marinate overnight in the fridge.

STEP 4

If you want to barbecue your chicken, get the coals burning 1 hr or so before you're ready to cook. Authentic jerked meats are not exactly grilled as we think of grilling, but sort of smoke-grilled. To get a more authentic jerk experience, add some wood chips to your barbecue, and cook your chicken over slow, indirect heat for 30 mins.

STEP 5

To cook in the oven, heat to 180C/160C fan/gas 4. Put the chicken pieces in a roasting tin with the halved lime and cook for 45 mins until tender and cooked through.

STEP 6

While the chicken is cooking, prepare the rice & peas. Rinse the basmati rice in plenty of cold water, then tip it into a large saucepan. Add the coconut milk, spring onions, thyme sprigs, garlic and ground allspice.

STEP 7

Season with salt, add 300ml cold water and set over a high heat. Once the rice begins to boil, turn it down to a medium heat, cover and cook for 10 mins. Add the kidney beans to the rice, then cover with a lid. Leave off the heat for 5 mins until all the liquid is absorbed.

STEP 8

Squeeze the roasted lime over the chicken and serve with the rice & peas, and some hot sauce if you like it really spicy.

Jerk sweet potato & black bean curry

Ingredients

- 2 onions, 1 diced, 1 roughly chopped
- 2 tbsp sunflower oil
- 50g ginger, roughly chopped
- small bunch coriander, leaves and stalks separated
- 3 tbsp jerk seasoning
- 2 thyme sprigs
- 400g can chopped tomato
- 4 tbsp red wine vinegar
- 3 tbsp demerara sugar
- 2 vegetable stock cubes, crumbled
- 1kg sweet potato, peeled and cut into chunks
- 2 x 400g cans black beans, rinsed and drained

- 450g jar roasted red pepper, cut into thick slices

Method

STEP 1

Gently soften the diced onion in the sunflower oil in a big pan or casserole.

STEP 2

Meanwhile, whizz together the roughly chopped onion, ginger, coriander stalks and jerk seasoning with a hand-held blender. Add to the softened onion and fry until fragrant. Stir in the thyme, chopped tomatoes, vinegar, sugar and stock cubes with 600ml water and bring to a simmer. Simmer for 10 mins, then drop in the sweet potatoes and simmer for 10 mins more. Stir in the beans, peppers and some seasoning, and simmer for another 5 mins until the potatoes are almost tender. Cool and chill for up to 2 days.

STEP 3

To serve, gently heat through on the hob. Roughly chop most of the coriander leaves and stir in, then serve scattered with the remaining leaves.

Jerk beefburger with pineapple relish & chips

Ingredients

- 4 very large potatoes
- 1 tbsp vegetable oil
- 1 red onion , ½ grated and ½ finely chopped
- 1 carrot , grated
- 400g/ 14oz beef mince
- 2 tsp jerk seasoning (we used Bart)
- 200g/7oz fresh pineapple (we used pre-cut packet), finely chopped
- 1 red chilli , deseeded and finely chopped

- small handful coriander , roughly chopped
- juice 1 lime
- lettuce and burger buns , to serve

Method

STEP 1

Heat oven to 190C/170C fan/gas 5. Scrub the potatoes and cut into chips. Lay the chips in a single layer on a baking tray, drizzle with oil, season and toss to coat. Bake for 40 mins until crisp.

STEP 2

Mix together the grated onion, carrot, mince and jerk seasoning in a large bowl, then shape into 4 evenly sized patties.

STEP 3

Heat a non-stick frying pan till hot, then cook the burgers for 5-6 mins each side.

STEP 4

To make the relish, mix the chopped onion, pineapple, chilli, coriander and lime juice. To serve, place the burgers in split buns with some lettuce and the spicy relish. Serve with the crispy chips.

GOES WELL WITH

Lemony rice & peas

Cheese & chive coleslaw

www.ingramcontent.com/pod-product-compliance
Lightning Source LLC
Chambersburg PA
CBHW061337120726
48001CB00002B/916